DARKNESS
TO LIGHT
1 PETER 2:9

ISBN   Paperback: 979-8-9933665-0-0
ISBN   Hardback: 979-8-9933665-1-7
ISBN   eBook: 979-8-9933665-2-4

Library of Congress Control Number:

Published By:

BOOKMARC
A L L I A N C E

DARKNESS TO LIGHT

1 PETER 2:9

LINET ONDUSO

CONTENTS

DEDICATION

To my family and precious children. My two princes Ed and Edi, my beautiful princess B and my lovely mother. And to all those who will get a chance to purchase the book....

ACKNOWLEDGEMENTS

I would like to acknowledge God, for his grace, mercy, righteousness, salvation and redemption. For being so faithful to his promises and opening doors that I knew nothing about. My children and family for supporting me in times of trials, even when I failed them repeatedly. For never giving up on me. My Aunt Robai, thank you for believing and pushing me to become a better person.

Leaders of Gospel Power Church, Rev Renson and Pastor Redempter Duka, for your mentorship and for being my Spiritual parents. For endless prayers during my trial seasons. Smart ministries, Pastor Robert Odanga and Pastor Jackie Odanga, what can I say; other than I'm very grateful. For being genuine and authentic in spirit, for remaining vigilant and gallant and for standing strong. Thank you for welcoming me with open arms and accepting me for who I am. This far is because of your encouragement and support.

I would also love to thank Alianza DV, Carmen Nieves, Jocelyn Martinez, Margie Quinones and the entire team for helping me grow and giving me a chance to be part of the Alianza team. Thank you

Finally, called Coach Academy; thank you for the lessons and for helping me become a spiritual and transformational coach. Lastly, Hanna and Elsa from book publishing, for your dedication, effort and patience. I appreciate you all. Thank you so much, without you, this would not be it.

And to my church, my family, my home; Gospel Power Center, Oregon. Bishop Ben Mwangi and Rev Jane Mwangi, Pastor Peter, for all you have done and continue to do I acknowledge you from the deepest part of my heart. With heartfelt gratitude I say thank you and may the good Lord continue to keep and protect you.

ABOUT THE AUTHOR

Linet Onduso is a good example of what a walking and living testimony looks like. Born in Kenya and raised in the USA, with 3 beautiful children.

Linet is a Minister of the Gospel, an author, a publisher, a counselor, a speaker and a certified Christian Life Coach. To schedule for consultation of any of the above services, please send her a message on her website,

https://vesselsofthekingdom.com/,

Linet has a founder of
h**ttps://vesselsofthekingdom.com/.**

Vessels Of the Kingdom or
https://paperbell.me/linet-onduso-1.

She also owns **Linet Onduso Publishing and Literary Firm.**

VAGABOND

I thought I was meant to be spoiled and pampered, since I was the only girl, with my two younger brothers, but that was not the case. My mother was a woman who loved us equally, but of course, I did not see that love back then. Instead, all I saw was hate from my family, and that made me rebellious. I became a runaway child who preferred to stay with friends and people I knew nothing about instead of my own blood. But also, they never made it easy for me, so every time I missed home and came back, I would get a whooping of my life. My brothers and family members treated me like I was a plague. Seemed like I had a disease that was infectious enough that sometimes, I would hear my aunts telling my cousins not to play or mingle with me.

It's not to brag but to say that even as a sinner, God still loved me and protected me, **Romans 5:8**, *but God His own love toward us, in that while we were still sinners. Christ died for us.*

Ephesians 2:4, *But God who is rich in mercy, because of his great love with which he loved us, [5]even when we were dead in trespasses, made us alive together with Christ (By grace you have been saved),*

Why do I say that? I was born and raised in a middle-class family, which means that our lives were not bad. God was making way and providing for us. In my late teens, I started becoming rebellious, as I mentioned earlier. My family became my worst enemy; there was nothing my mom didn't try to do in the name of seeking help for me.

I remember being taken to different places for witchcraft, drinking portions, and my body being cut by sharp razor blades and rubbing things in those wounds and told to say some incantations out loud. I have those marks on my body till date. They would even cut my tongue and head. Or they would ask me to go on a junction road at 3 am, throw an egg or a black chicken.

They would ask me to drink some stuff, take dry black powders, and put stuff in my bathing water before I had my bath while saying some incantations. I was involved in a lot of rituals by sorcerers and warlocks. My mom went from city to village trying to seek help; now that I think about it, I'm like, why didn't she ever try church, right? The Bible says that *"the thief only came to steal, kill and destroy; I have come that they may have life and have it to the full"* **John 10:10.**

He did exactly that; he stole my joy, peace, and love. He tried to kill my inner spirit, soul and destroy my sanity.

Now that I have my own child, I can't even imagine the pain my mom went through. As young as I was, I didn't know any better; I'm not sure if I was looking to fit in or be accepted. I always felt that my friends and their families treated me better than my own, and using that as a weapon, I was out in the wilderness more than I was with my family. Satan stole all my teenage life and took advantage of it. The places I left my home to stay were worse than poverty itself. I remember once I went to stay with one of my cousins; though I did not know her well, I knew that my mom would not be able to find me there, no matter how hard she looked for me.

My cousin was so poor even the mice complained. They lived in ancient days when a mattress to sleep on was a waste of money, and they had one horrible meal a day and never had soap. My cousin would have loved to kick me out because they could not afford to feed another extra mouth. But instead of kicking me out, she started using me for her gain. She would connect me with the men around the neighborhood who were a little better off to give her money, food, or traditional alcohol for my exchange. Trust me, I was very young. I easily accepted that life because I knew my family hated me and never wanted anything to do with me, so I was better off out there. I held on to alcohol as my dear best friend, so being with these men never bothered me, when I was drunk, though I contracted various sexual diseases. Alcohol numbed my pain!

Before deciding to go to my cousin's place or to find this place, I tried to stay in the capital city, but that did not turn out well for me. The only way I could find a place to stay was if I befriended the bus or minibus conductors. I knew how to do that because whenever my mom would send me to school, which was a boarding school, I would link up with them, and instead of going to school, I chose to hang out with them, got drunk, and involved myself in sexual immorality.

It's sad when I write about it now because my mom used to struggle a lot. She made sure that we went to good schools; not only that, but they were very expensive. Whenever she would come to see me, that's when she would find out that I had not been in school for months. You cannot blame her; there were no cell phones back then, and house phones were not popular either. Anyways yeah, that's how I became popular with the bus conductors.

One time, while out there with nowhere to go, I met a girl almost my age. It was getting very late, and I knew that that night, it was not possible for me to find a place to sleep, since all my usuals had gone out of town or home with their wives. This girl was like a lifesaver; she told me that she knew someone who would give us a place to sleep if I was willing to follow her. I agreed, and we left with the male person she was talking about.

I was not suspicious of anything because I thought that she was going through a similar situation to me. When we got to our destination, where the man lived, I found out that the girl had set me up; it was her job to find young girls and invite them over, but she got paid and abandoned you there. At this time, I couldn't escape because there wasn't just one guy but seven guys waiting for me. They raped me one at a time till they were done, then threw me out like a dog. The pain, the guilt, the hurt, yet I still couldn't go home.

Who would believe me anyway?

I could not blame anyone for my misfortune, yet I blamed my mom for not loving me enough, for hating me so much that I had to go through that incident. Believers, trust me: when the devil is aware of your destiny, he will use every method to stop your destiny from coming true. In this matter, he used my family. To tell the truth, I did not have a good relationship with anyone, not a single soul in my family. I had an uncle, my mom's brother. He is dead now, but when he was alive, they would swear that he was the only one who loved me. The reason was that every time I ran from home, he was the one who would go in search of me.

No one knew the truth behind it; he could not stand seeing me with any other man because he was the one who used to rape me. Did I tell my mom, grandma, or family? Definitely NO. They never would have believed me because of who I was back then, but also because everyone was afraid of my uncle. He used to beat any man who would try to come close to me, pretending that he was responsible and wanted the best for me.

Through all this mess, I desired death so bad, and since I felt like I was already dead inside. There was a time when I returned home with the goal of killing myself. I did not want to do it where my family couldn't find my body, and so the best option was to commit suicide at home.

When I got home, I gave it a few days, and then, one night, I made up my mind. Yes, I was ready to go. I'm still not sure how death came as an option because I was still young and hadn't witnessed death or knew much about death and did not know much about God either because growing up, the church was just a routine thing, like a culture.

You only go to church because it's Sunday and not for God's word or presence. It's safe to say we were churchgoers who went on special occasions like Christmas. We were not dedicated or baptized in church and had no close relationship with the church either.

I had no guilt of going to hell or heaven if I committed suicide, since I had not been taught about the afterlife and the consequences of hanging on a tree. We were not a religious family; my dad was an alcoholic who spent most of his time at work and in the bar. That night, I waited till everyone went to bed; I took malaria pills called chloroquine, went to the bathroom, and swallowed them, then went to bed knowing I wasn't going to wake up ever again. I was not scared to die, because I didn't know death.

Around midnight, I was woken up by a sharp stomach pain, ran to the bathroom, and behold, I started throwing up the pills, sixty-two in total. Taking them was much easier than them coming out.

Did I learn anything from that incident? I wish I could say yes, but no, I did not. In fact, I was determined to find a better, easier, and quicker way of committing suicide. About a month or two later, I left home again, and this time went to one of my other cousins. All these cousins were from my mother's side. At her place, I was tortured by different men, abused, bruised, and left with an STD. On one occasion, I will never forget this, I get flashes in my mind. One time, when I had just returned home and had a huge disagreement with one of my brothers, which was nothing new to my mom, my siblings fought, and so was the case with my brother. But this time, it was different; while fighting, he punched me in the stomach; nothing happened at that moment, but in anger, I took some of my clothes and left. Yes, I had a spirit of anger/temper; my mom was still at work, so no one could stop me from leaving.

I went to my so-called boyfriend and told him what happened. Not that it was a big deal because my family never liked him, they thought he was the reason I kept running away from home and he was poor. That night, for some reason, I was unable to sleep; I had severe stomach pains that could not be stopped by anything. Felt like my abdomen was being crushed.

When it was dawn, my boyfriend left for work as usual, and a few minutes later, the pain intensified, and suddenly, I felt like something was reaping my uterus. Being young and confused, I took a mirror and looked down there, and Lord, behold, I saw hairs on like a head. I couldn't really tell what it was because I had never been pregnant before and did not know that I was pregnant. I got so scared, and I did the unimaginable; I pushed whatever was back into my tummy, and I ran outside the apartment, knocking on the neighbors' doors for help.

It was a holiday on that day, so everyone was in their homes; in addition, it was raining heavily and early in the morning. One of the neighbors was kind enough to direct me to a midwife who was about thirty minutes away. Those days, there was no Uber, so I had to either run or walk. From my story, you can tell that I wasn't in one of the good areas of the city. On my way to the midwife, I started bleeding; the rain and the blood were creating a good flow that dripped from me. I honestly couldn't even process what and how I was pregnant.

I got to the midwife's place and knocked on her door while screaming in pain. She didn't open it, but one of her neighbors came out and told me that the midwife had travelled to her village for the holidays. It was December when everyone was getting ready for Christmas. I was left with no other option but to go to my boyfriend's brother, who lived twenty minutes away from the midwife's place. The bleeding was becoming too much, but I made it there with the grace of God. I knocked on his door, and when he opened, I took my first step through the door, and the baby dropped and hit the cement floor. I passed out, and when I regained consciousness, my boyfriend was beside me in a taxi heading to the hospital.

Apparently, his brother had called him, and he left work immediately and came over. The hospital he took me to could not do much for me because the baby was already out. It was only for mothers who were about to deliver, so they sent us to another hospital. My boyfriend had to call my parents and ask for help because he had used all the money, he had accumulated that morning in the taxi and the bed sheets he had bought to cover me and stop the blood from getting on the car seats. I will never forget the look on my mom's face when they came; I recall my mom throwing a coin to my boyfriend so that he could take a bus back home. She and my dad took me to the hospital they had referred me to so that they could clean my stomach.

Besides all, my parents did not abandon me; they did take me there. I was admitted for a few days and scheduled for the cleaning. Ladies, let me tell you, I will choose the pain of a miscarriage over the pain you go through while they clean your womb. First, they do not administer any medications for pain, and during the entire process, there is no medicine. They explained that it's another method to remind young girls never to repeat it. No anesthesia, no ivy, or any painkillers. They part your legs wide and insert the machine. You get to feel every move they make in your stomach. So, get this, after going through that pain, my stomach was cleaned three more times. And you would think the pain is a lesson not to have sex or get pregnant.

Later, my boyfriend told me that the baby was full-term, and she was a girl. Sadly, they had nowhere to bury her, so they dug a hole in the neighborhood, where people threw their trash and put her there. It was not even a grave, no casket, just wrapped her and threw her like that, or should I say disposed of her. I can't really blame anyone but Satan, who stole my little girl from me. People bury their pets, but I could not afford to bury my nine-month-old child. Doesn't that tell you that the devil is a big liar? I was grateful though; I did not have a special bond with her, nor did I know I was carrying her. I did not see her face, so it was easy for me to forget the pain and move on.

ROCK BOTTOM AND BEYOND

I was done with life in general and believed that everything they said about me was true. I finally agreed with those who said I was a curse in my family, because I did not see any other relative going through what I was going through. I believed that when they said I would not amount to anything, they were right because every choice I made seemed very wrong, with horrible outcomes. I could not even do the easy job of carrying a child in my womb for nine months. I was good for nothing.

That's when a thought crossed my mind that at home, I was not successful with the suicide because my family was not supposed to see me dead. And so, at my cousins, I tried hanging myself using a rope at my cousins' house. There were two things I didn't do enough research on hanging, so I didn't know how to tie the rope. The second reason was that God was not done with me yet. *Galatians 3:13* says, *"Christ has redeemed us from the curse of the law, having become a curse for us (for it is written, "Cursed is everyone who hangs on a tree")*

I slowed the pace of my ignorance and pride, but still, things kept happening to me, like having four miscarriages, and my first child being born prematurely. This one, I had to stay in the hospital for three good months. That's when I started understanding things of God a little. My son was one of those miracles that will make you call on God. He was born prematurely due to pneumonia; I remember this like it was yesterday. Since he was very premature, he had to be incubated, and because he couldn't breastfeed on his own, I had to feed him through the syringe, 2 ml every two hours day and night.

It was so by the grace of God that he made it, and he is alive today. Because they couldn't give him any medication, we just had to wait on God. There were days when he would faint due to fever. One day, I remember in the process of him fainting, the nurse called me and told me, *"Hey, come check your thing is dying, just so you don't say we killed it,"* were her exact words. Sometimes, I wonder, as a woman, how you can have the audacity to say such words to another woman or if it was just another way for me to hold onto God.

That was the first time I ever called on God and told him to have mercy on me. I asked God to help me not leave the hospital without my child after everything I was going and had gone through. God answered my prayers, and my son lived.

Leaving the hospital, I found out that his father was getting money from my family to bring it to me, but instead, he got himself a new girlfriend on whom he was spending the money. He even dared to give his girlfriend my clothes as gifts, got her pregnant, and moved her into my apartment. When he heard that I was being discharged, he went and asked my grandma for money so that we could move everything to a portion of land my mom had purchased. His game was for me not to come and find another woman in my apartment. But as the word of God says, nothing can be hidden; truth will always come out.

Those who knew me had already gossiped about it to me, and told me how he even sold my sewing machine and television to sustain their needs. Just because I had my son didn't mean that I had become a saint. Everyone knew me in that city, so I had people who already had information about this girl and where she lived. I played it quietly for a few days, and then finally, I went to visit the new woman in my man's life. She wasn't far from my place, so it was not that hard to find her. And I had good intel and excellent paparazzi as well. I got to their house, introduced myself, and asked for my clothes. She only gave me one skirt, and I remember getting so mad because that skirt was not only my favorite, but my mom bought it for me.

The good thing is that I had come prepared, so I locked her and her mom in the house, poured gasoline on it, and tried to burn them down. Relax, they survived the fire; a good neighbor opened the door for them, and they were able to escape. She did not learn from it, and so the next time I got her with my baby daddy, I decided to teach her a lesson she would never forget. Not only did I pour acid on her, but I also beat her so badly that she lost the pregnancy. That was the end of my relationship with my baby daddy, and I never heard about that woman again. To tell you the truth, I have no idea what happened to her or where she went after that. All I know is that baby daddy didn't settle down with her but another woman. And please just defend myself; I was not saved and delivered then, so the devil had the upper hand. I enjoyed being called a bad girl;

I treasured pain at all costs. Making someone suffer was my joy, my pride.

Let's continue; this is all about me and no one else. I am only trying to explain what the devil put me through before Jesus found me. Life went on, I went back home, stayed with my son for a few months, then left him with mom and went back to the world. This time, it was different; I first went to my mom's farm, harvested all the corn, and sold it. God, I had a good amount of cash and moved to another city, got me an apartment and a few house items, and looked for a job. I am not sure if I mentioned earlier that I was a home wrecker as I entered another relationship with a married man. I knew very well that he was married, but because I felt joy in other people's misery, I made sure that his wife left him. Now I know that I had the spirit of destruction or the python spirit.

I had another child with him while working as a bartender. I quit the job and went to stay at my grandmother's place, after making sure that his wife had abandoned him. By then, my mom had seriously used a lot of resources on me. She wanted the best out of me, but because Satan had blinded me, I didn't see love but hatred. I was Satan's loyal servant; it didn't matter how hard it looked, I would dare people for being a very good home wrecker, and I was proud of it. I went to the extent of dating a pastor just because I wanted to prove that even a praying man could not resist me. And I did break that home, which resulted in that Pastor committing suicide, not because of the broken home but because I rejected him later. He was very willing to leave his church and ministry just to be with me, but because it was only a game to me; I was not ready for the outcome.

I think about it all now, and it breaks my heart because of how much pain I caused to parents, their children, families, and their children. Back then, I did not care how people saw me or what they said about me. Why? Because I was already used to hearing all that from my family, it was nothing new to me. I used to say that if their talk did not remove any bone from me or bruise my flesh, then I was good. Oh, how I also loved to fight, so no one dared me or had enough courage because they knew the end results of the people, I fought with were never good. I was in my own small world of your own business.

It hurts that I had no one to lead me to Jesus, deliverance, and salvation. I went through a lot of abuse, especially sexual abuse, until I became immune to it. It didn't hurt me anymore. I took it as a means of survival. I knew I had something to exchange for what I wanted, like somewhere to sleep, food, or a nice warm bed. Can you believe someone raped me so that I could sleep in an unfinished building? I would love to point fingers and play the blame game, but from what I know now, I had the spirit of prostitution in me. It's either I became the devil's pet, or I just worked overtime for him with no benefits.

I worked as a housekeeper/cleaner for some woman, yet in our own home, we had a hired housekeeper. That job did not last for long because I was not used to being told what to do. The only reason I did it was because the woman, my employer, used to sell alcohol that I had access to. Now that I think about it, I can't remember when I was ever sober, and because of my addiction to alcohol, I couldn't stay home. While out there, in the wilderness, I used to get sick a lot, be arrested a lot, and fight a lot. I had a very quick temper, and if I put my hands on you, I made sure I damaged you.

Fast forward, God showed me a favor and opened doors for me to travel out of the country as an exchange student. It's true when people say that no one can stop your destiny. It can be delayed but not denied. What God has for you, is meant for you, and no one else can take it away. You may know it and use it to live your purpose or fail to realize it and live a wasted life. I recall when we went to get my visa, by we, I mean me and my dad; we had to be up by 4:00 am, and when we got there around 6:00 am, there was already a long queue of about one hundred people ahead of us.

On that day, they denied me the visa, stating that they did not have enough details about the exchange program, so I went back home and left for my mother's village in a few days. About three days later, my cousin came by and told me that I was needed in the city ASAP; and that I had to go back to the embassy. I asked him what had happened. He said that the American consular called the embassy and told them that I had to be in USA immediately.

If that was not God opening doors for me, then I don't know who else.

My goal for returning to the village was to get married at that young age and just take care of my second child. I had no dreams or goals planned; I didn't know how I was going to make it, but my mind was made up on trying it. So, my cousin came at the right time, why? Because if I had left, I don't think my family would have been able to find me for that opportunity again.

I went back and got the visa, but when we got back home, I realized that my visa would expire two months before my departure date. It was to expire in March when my departure was in August. That meant I had to go back to the embassy for them to fix it; in a way, I would get relieved, hoping I was not going so that I could raise my son, but my other hope was to go so that I could give them the best life they ever had. I was torn between two options because by then, my mom had already travelled, and I couldn't imagine my young babies without their grandmother or me.

Satan tried to throw punches at me, but God fought my battles. God had a better plan for my life, just like he has said in *Jeremiah 29:11: For I know the plans I have for you, declares the Lord, plans to prosper you and not to harm you, plans to give you hope and a future."*

As an exchange student, I went back to eleventh grade, where I had dropped out while in Africa. I graduated and got my diploma. During this period, I had toned down many of my problematic behaviors. Although I still indulged in a bit of mischief, I was careful to avoid actions that might land me in trouble. Since I was in a new country with unique cultural norms, I had to respect and adapt to their ways as part of my experience as an exchange student. It wasn't just me making these changes; I could sense that it was God reaching out to me, steadily guiding me toward a better path.

I graduated and moved to another state where my family lived; and moved in with my aunt. And behold, I started drifting back to my old ways. My aunt was very strict and never for a minute could be played around. I became very stubborn. One day, she got tired of me and asked me to move out because it was her house, and of course, she had rules. She came home and gave me resources for the shelter and told me to start calling to get space because it filled up fast. I thought she was joking until I went out on my first date to watch a movie.

One of her strict house rules was that if you weren't employed, you had to be home by 9:00 pm. Unfortunately, the movie I watched ran late, and I didn't make it back until after 10:00 pm. When I rang the doorbell, it was the homeowner herself who answered. Without a word, she held out her hand, asking for the house keys, and then told me to come back on the weekend to collect my things. That marked the beginning of my life on my own, and things started spiraling from there. It was as if life had decided to teach me some harsh lessons.

THE SPIRIT OF ADDICTION

I went from just drinking to becoming a professional drinker, meaning I could never get drunk and knew what liquor to take. I knew what drink I needed when I was happy or ready to fight. I was not a beer person, really. Guinness was the only beer I could drink, but then it had to go with Tequila Jose Gold. I would drink any silver drink, especially Patron. I used to buy the little nips and carry them everywhere with me, including work. I would pour the liquor into a coffee mug and just sip it at my workplace with no issues. My backpack, glove compartment, on the side doors of my car never ever lacked alcohol.

In the house, I made sure I had a bar with enough stock just in case I got broke, which I was most of the time, because I used to spend almost $700 a month on alcohol. I would not even fix my car; instead, I would just drink, which caused me to get arrested a lot. I have been arrested in almost every city county jail due to a suspended license or rejection sticker. Only once did they find me with an open bottle of liquor and charge me $500.

I'm sure by now you can't tell that the devil was robbing me of all my sweat through my wrong choices. In case I was drunk enough for the police to smell it if they pulled me over, I would always have garlic and sardines in my car.

I remember once the cops pulled me over because of overspeeding, and when he got to my car, I opened the can of sardines, and my entire car had a nasty stinge. The officer asked me what the smell was from, and I told him it was my lunch. He was about to throw up, so he let me go. Since then, that can have to be in my car. This other time, I went out of town for a party, and then had to drive back after 2 am.

For some reason, I missed my exit, and instead of going forward to the next exit, I decided to reverse on a highway. For some reason, someone saw me and called the state trooper. He pulled me over after I had already taken my exit, and his question was," Do you know why I pulled you over?"

"No officer. Any problem?" I asked.

"Were you the one who just reversed on the Highway? We received an alert."

"No way officer, me? No, there's no way I can do such a crazy thing. I do love my life very much."

Believe it or not, Satan can make a lie look so good. He believed me and let me go. Later, When I think about that incident, I could have been hurt or caused a horrible accident. Okay, this other time, I woke up early with a hangover, and because I was late for work, I decided that I was not going to let my car run for a while to melt the frost. I hopped in and drove off with a frosted windshield. The next thing I remember is I tried to make a right turn, and my car ended up hanging on an electrical pole.

I had to crawl out through the window and call 911. When they came, they couldn't figure out how it happened, but they had to cut some wires to get it down. And I paid a huge fine for destroying government property. *Alcohol was not a good friend*, as I thought. All it did was make me spend more money paying fines. When you are addicted to anything, you will do anything and everything to have it. I used to buy alcohol or credit or even go to clubs to drink and pay later. My kidneys became a concern to my doctor for a while because the liquor was affecting them. So, not only was I wasting money, but ruining my health.

Another thing that alcohol was doing to my health is that I went through a season of continuous flow of blood for about six months. The doctors could not figure out what caused it. I started taking birth control pills not for family planning but to stop my menstrual flow. My health became a mess, I was very insecure, and most of my other finances went to purchasing hygiene products. My down there became so bruised from trying to use all sorts of products. Eventually, my doctor found a shot that was able to stop it; the reason for all that was because of my earlier sexual experiences. Ladies, be careful with what you participate in during intimacy.

I was clubbing Thursday-Saturday, then Sunday to deal with the hangover. I worked a lot, but I was always poor. Remember, earlier when I said the devil came to steal, I always worked two or three jobs but had no money, no savings. I was very ignorant of traffic laws. The times I got arrested were always because of a rejected inspection sticker on the car or a suspended license. Whenever I would take my car for inspection, and it failed, I never bothered to fix it, till I got arrested. My family got tired of bailing me out but was always worried about my whereabouts. As an alcoholic, I became suicidal again, and I used to try it while driving, especially when I got angry; I would head the car straight to the Curb or drive at a very high speed with the hopes of swerving off the road, flip couple of times and die. A little craziness continued here and there until the year 2015.

BROKEN TRUST

I met a very handsome man at a club I frequented. He approached me, and we chatted for a while. We exchanged numbers, and I got to know him as Mr. Blessing. At that time, I wasn't very interested in him because I had someone else, not a boyfriend, but one of my "cooling stations" or "one for the road" type of guys. A few days later, Mr. Blessing reached out, and once we started talking, we became inseparable, like magnets. It was a good feeling because I thought he was the first person to shower me with so much affection.

However, after a few months, I noticed some behaviors that didn't sit well with me. Mr. Blessing became obsessed with me; he would show up at my place without letting me know, and if I didn't answer his calls, he'd start calling everyone I was related to. We began having disagreements, and physical fights occurred frequently.

I remember one incident after an argument when he tried to make it up to me by inviting me to dinner. When I arrived at the restaurant, he was already there, and we ordered drinks as usual. Before the meal, he told me he had a gift for me. I was excited because he was usually good at picking out things I liked. He went to his car and came back with a gift bag. Inside the bag were all the text messages I had sent to my friends and family. Although they contained nothing inappropriate, because they were in a language he didn't understand, he considered it a problem.

I ask you: what kind of man wakes up in the middle of the night, screenshots all the texts on your phone, prints them out, and then hands them to you for translation and clarification?

We never got a chance to eat our dinner because I was furious. When I tried to leave the restaurant, he dragged me back and started punching me. He took my car keys and wouldn't let me get into my car. Why? Because he wanted me to translate all the texts I had written in my language. A good Samaritan saw what was happening and came to help me, but Mr. Blessing assumed that this person was my boyfriend—why else would anyone interfere in someone else's business? At least, that's what he thought. The Samaritan called the police, and as soon as Mr. Blessing heard the sirens, he left, throwing the keys at me on his way out.

I'm sure you would think that after that incident, the relationship would end, especially since he physically assaulted me. But it didn't. Not even close. Talk about ignoring red flags.

I drove home in a fury, venting to my best friend on the phone the entire way. A week later, Mr. Blessing came over, and we patched things up. Since he hadn't mentioned he was coming over, I had picked up an extra shift at work, so I had to leave early the next morning. As I was leaving the house, he suddenly jumped into the passenger seat. I asked him what he was doing, and he replied that he was going wherever I was going. I thought he was bluffing until he actually hopped into the moving car. I told myself that once I got to work, he would realize I was telling the truth and leave. But to my surprise, he didn't budge.

If I were my own boss, I would have fired myself for bringing him to work. It was incredibly embarrassing, especially because I worked in a group home. One of my coworkers, who was a bit older than me, suggested I end the relationship before things got out of hand. He was right.

I didn't initially see what my coworker saw, but yes, things began to get worse every day. We have an African saying: "What an old person sees while sitting, a young child cannot see even while standing." We fought every time we were together, whether at home or in public. And when I say "fight," I mean physical, Mike Tyson-style fistfights. We gave each other plenty of bruises and scars. This was not even six months into the relationship.

At my job, I was a supervisor, which meant I was in constant communication with the director of the group home. One day, my boyfriend took an intimate picture of us while we were sleeping and sent it to my boss, demanding he leave me alone because I was his girlfriend—and threatening to tell the boss's wife if he didn't comply. My boss called me into his office on a Monday morning and showed me the picture. I was humiliated and furious. When I confronted my boyfriend, he said he didn't like the way my boss and I worked together. I couldn't bear the shame, so I quit my job.

I wish I could say that was the end of it, but there were many more incidents. He befriended all my friends on social media and sent them messages asking how they knew me or how we were related. This included my coworkers. As a result, I lost many friends and felt too guilty to tell my family. I used to be very private about my personal relationships, but that didn't last long. Because of our constant disagreements, he would run to my family before I had a chance to explain things. My family called meetings to address the issues, but nothing improved. The abuse, stalking, and cheating became too much.

The final straw was when he started stalking me and my mom. He would follow us everywhere, just because I wasn't spending enough time with him.

I was exhausted and felt like I had no one to talk to; Blessing had made sure I was isolated, with only him around. The final straw came when we went out on New Year's Day. He insisted that we should go out and start the year with a positive vibe, and he knew I loved reggae music. While at the club, he ordered a drink that he shouldn't have, because he couldn't handle alcohol. He always tried to prove himself, but he had a low tolerance, just like I did.

That night, I had a gut feeling that something was going to go wrong, so I mentally prepared myself for what might happen. I wasn't sure exactly how or when his outburst would occur, but I knew I needed to be ready. I ordered a Long Island iced tea, a strong drink that I rarely had. He asked for the same drink, and the bartender, who knew me because I had been a regular there for over ten years, gave me a warning look, as if to say, "Cool it." I had also worked as a DJ at the same place for about two years, so I had some rapport with the staff.

After a few sips, he suddenly wanted to dance, but I declined because the song playing wasn't my style. He went to the bathroom, and when he returned, he grabbed me by the collar and started dragging me outside. Mind you, I was sitting on a high stool at the time. The security guards, who knew me well, asked if I needed help, but I told them I could handle it and that I'd sort it out. Blessing was the type of person who wouldn't back off or walk away to cool down; he would stay in your face until he ran out of steam.

I got into the car with him, and after we had driven a short distance from the club, I grabbed the steering wheel and pulled the car over to the curb.

For almost a year, I let this man abuse, misuse, and demean me. I lost my self-image and my sense of identity, and nothing made sense anymore. However, I had done a good job of not fighting back, even though I knew how. Why? Because I was afraid of what I might do to him if I fought back. Truth be told, he didn't intimidate me—I grew up with brothers, and we fought day and night. I knew I could handle him because I had never lost a fight before, but I was afraid of the damage I could cause if I unleashed my full force. But that night, I was ready. He wouldn't know what hit him.

He was driving, so I pulled the steering wheel hard to the side. He stopped the car, ready to throw a punch as usual, but this time, I was the one delivering the punches. Before he could even react, blood was dripping from his nose, and his lip was split open. I got out of the car and started walking down the sidewalk. It was about two am. A young woman who had just left the club saw me by the curb and offered me a ride home. I thought that Blessing would use the drive home to cool off and think things over, but no. He showed up at my place, ready to finish what I had started. I was prepared—I wasn't backing off this time.

He tried to grab me, but I dodged and then pinned him down. I started throwing punches, letting out all my pent-up rage. He managed to grab my arm and bit my wrist. I still have the scar from that bite, a permanent reminder of that night.

The bite mark was the least of my worries. I managed to subdue him, and when he couldn't fight anymore, I put my foot on his neck and called 911. When the dispatcher answered, my words were, "You better come and take my fingerprints because I'm about to kill him." The police arrived in less than three minutes. They asked what happened, and I explained everything from start to finish. They asked if I wanted him to leave the premises, and I said yes. Once he was gone, they suggested I get a restraining order. He lived about an hour away, so I thought I wouldn't see him for a while. But I was wrong.

Later that evening, my family called me and asked me to come over. They told me that he had visited them, wearing a shirt covered in blood, and claimed that I had beaten him. I told my family that I didn't want to talk about it and never wanted to see him again.

A few weeks later, after some soul-searching, I realized this wasn't the kind of relationship I wanted. I knew I deserved better and decided to let go of the toxic relationship. Around the same time, Blessing disguised himself as someone else, using a different phone number, and tried to flirt with me. I rejected him, but instead of taking it like a grown man, he ran to my family with printed texts of our brief conversation, claiming that I was already talking to another man. That's when my family realized he was a psychopath. They told him to give me space, and he lost it. He then threatened that I would regret rejecting him because I had no idea what he could do. Though I was alarmed, I wasn't overly worried since I knew how to defend myself. Nevertheless, I went to the local police and filed a report, just in case he followed through on his threats.

A MOTHER'S STRENGTH

A few weeks later, while I was in the process of closing that chapter, I found out I was a few weeks pregnant. Come on now, seriously, why? As a decent person, I felt the humane thing to do was to tell him I was carrying his child. His response was, "If I'm not going to be involved in the child's life, then have an abortion." How stupid! Whose body is it, his or mine? For the sake of my child, I allowed him to be involved, but nothing changed during the pregnancy. The arguments and the abuse continued. Some nights, I would sit outside in the cold, even during winter, because I didn't want the toxicity to affect my child.

It was not a smooth pregnancy; I was in and out of the hospital every week. I am grateful to my mom, who stopped everything to support me. Because of depression, I lost so much weight that people barely recognized me; you could only see the tiny bump on my belly. At six months, no one believed I was even one month pregnant. I couldn't sleep, I couldn't eat; all I did was throw up at everything, including the smell of my partner. My doctor prescribed an IV treatment every week because I was always dehydrated. I couldn't wait for my child to be born.

One day, after a disagreement, I left the house to go for a walk. During the walk, I remembered I had missed a midwife appointment, so I called to reschedule. They told me to come in on the same day, as I was close to my due date—I was 37 weeks pregnant. I returned to the apartment, took a shower, changed, and left without telling him where I was going.

A crucial point: Blessing had taken paternity leave from work without pay, but he spent the time playing video games. He didn't cook or do the dishes, so my mom used to bring me food, which he would eat as well.

I didn't see any reason to tell him my whereabouts either. An important thing to note is that my pregnancy prevented me from drinking. I tried to have a drink, especially with everything that was going on, but I couldn't even manage a sip. I bought all sorts of beer, wine, and liquor, trying to figure out which one might work, but my body rejected it all. My baby was transforming me for the better. I couldn't stand any smell related to alcohol without vomiting, and thankfully, I lost my taste for it. This was the longest period I'd been sober since I was maybe under ten years old. I didn't even know what sobriety felt like until I was pregnant.

When I got to the doctor, after taking my vitals, they told me I needed to be induced because I had pre-eclampsia. I felt like I was in a dream; I wanted my child so much, but I wasn't ready for this—it was too soon. I called my mom to bring me my hospital bag, and then I was off to the delivery room. My baby was stubborn about coming out, though, preferring the comfort of rent-free living. They first induced me with a balloon, which took a whole day to pop, and then the induction itself took almost two days. I was throwing up most of the time, while Blessing would come by to eat my food and sleep. He'd wake up in the morning, leave to watch sports and gamble, then come back later at night, eat my food, and sleep some more.

After almost three days, I had reached only three centimeters of dilation, and the doctors tried everything to ease my pain. Eventually, they decided I would need a C-section. Just as they were about to prep me, the doctor checked my dilation again, and there it was—the baby's head was starting to crown. With a single push, my life changed at that exact moment.

From that moment, nothing else mattered—I had a reason to live and fight for my DNA. My child became my motivation to keep going. Blessing was excited about the baby, taking every opportunity to snap photos and post them on social media. Unfortunately, that's all he seemed capable of doing for me and my child. He was full of envy and jealousy, and I can honestly say I've never met a worse father.

When I needed help with the baby, he was either incompetent or simply negligent. I lost count of how many times he nearly dropped our child. I don't know if I mentioned this, but during my pregnancy, I couldn't sleep. I would be awake all night and could only sleep for two hours in the morning. After the baby was born, it was the same thing. To make matters worse, my baby had colic, which meant constant crying and sleepless nights.

One night, I was walking around with my child and talking on the phone with an old friend. It was around midnight, and Blessing was, as usual, snoring on the couch like a broken radio. Suddenly, he came over and tried to snatch the baby from my arms. He had never shown interest in helping out at night, but now he was acting as if he wanted to be involved—by force. It was so typical of him to ignore the real responsibilities and then suddenly demand control over things he hadn't earned.

"Give me my child! You can't be talking to another man while holding my child!" Can you imagine? I refused to hand over the baby, and this turned into a heated argument that lasted all night. The next morning, I told him I was fed up with his behavior and that this wasn't how I wanted to raise my child. I asked him to move out. I explained that he could still see his child, but I didn't want him around me anymore because he was toxic. A word of advice, ladies: never let a man move in with you and add him to your lease, especially if he's not paying the bills or rent. Blessing refused and told me that since his name was on the lease, he wasn't going anywhere.

I had already made up my mind, so I found another apartment. I then called my landlord and told him I was moving out but that Blessing would stay and continue to pay the rent. I knew he couldn't afford it, but that wasn't my problem; he had made his choice. Eventually, Blessing came to his senses and agreed to move out, but by then, it was too late—I was leaving no matter what.

One evening, as he was taking his clothes, he suddenly claimed he might not be the father of my child. I said, "Okay, even better—

no need for you to come around, then." He probably thought I would beg him to stay, but I was so over him. My focus was my child, period.

When it was time for me to move, I left the old place with the baby because it was a cold winter day. My family was helping me with the move, and while I was at the new place, I heard his voice outside. I didn't want him to know my new address, but apparently, he showed up at the old place, claiming he came to help with the move. My family didn't see anything wrong with it, so they invited him along without asking me.

I settled in well at my new place, and Blessing began visiting on weekends, claiming he was there to see his child. The rule was that he would come, spend some time with the baby, and then leave, but he never stuck to that plan. Instead, he would bring his dirty laundry, do his washing while drinking, and then fall asleep drunk on the couch. He'd leave the next morning, having done nothing with the baby.

Moving forward, I decided to take my brothers on vacation. It had been a while since we'd had some peace of mind, so a trip seemed like a great idea. We drove for nine hours to North Carolina, and after checking into our rooms, I heard a knock at my door. I assumed it was room service or one of my brothers, but to my surprise, it was Blessing. How he found us, I had no idea, but he barged in, screaming about why I had left town with his child without informing him. The argument escalated quickly, and it turned physical. Blessing grabbed my three-month-old child, threw her onto the other side of the bed, and then pushed me out of the room, locking the door behind us. That's when it hit me—we were both outside the room with no keys, and my child was inside, screaming her lungs out.

First of all, my child wasn't feeling well; he had a cold, so his breathing wasn't good. I didn't know if he fell on the floor or onto the other bed when Blessing threw him. I ran downstairs to the reception, shaking, and asked for another room key. I also asked the receptionist to call the police. Blessing left before they got there, and my vacation abruptly ended. I drove back home, deciding to get a restraining order and to put him on child support.

I sent him a text explaining my intentions to do both, which I shouldn't have done. Ladies, here's some free advice: If you're done with a man and planning to take legal action, don't inform him of your plans. Just go ahead and do it. 99% of the time, he'll try to talk you out of it. No man wants to deal with the law.

And that's what Blessing did. He asked if we could talk about it first, and silly me, I agreed. We had arranged for him to come by on a specific day, but he didn't show. Instead, he turned up the next day. I will never forget that day—it was a Sunday, which was flea market day. I loved going to the flea market because my friends sold items from different cultures, and Blessing knew this because we used to go there when we were dating.

I didn't think much about it when he showed up and found me and my brothers on our way out. He said he wanted to come along, and we agreed, not knowing that he was already half-drunk.

He suggested we use his car, but a few miles down the highway, we all noticed that he was swerving. We asked him to take us back, but he refused and kept driving erratically. We then requested that he pull over so we could get an Uber, but he still refused and kept speeding. The arguing continued until a state trooper pulled us over. The officer explained that they pulled us over because several people had reported our car for reckless driving. Blessing was furious about getting a ticket and blamed me, claiming I was a horrible person because I didn't defend him.

We got to the flea market safely and walked around, but we were not speaking to each other and kept our distance. We went our separate ways in the market and met back at the car when we were done. In the car, Blessing pulled out two pocketknives he had bought at the flea market—one was black, and the other was pink. They looked like combs until you removed the covers. He proudly showed them off, saying he'd always wanted to own a knife. I wasn't too concerned because I also had a thing for knives.

FROM FALSE ACCUSATIONS TO
INCARCERATION

When we got home, it was getting late, so we called it a night. Blessing had to leave, and we went to bed because the next day was a school day. Before he left, Blessing took out the pink pocketknife, examined it, and said he had bought it for me. I thanked him and told him to put it on the counter, out of reach of the baby, who was at the age of grabbing things.

Blessing said he was going to sleep on the couch, then leave once he sobered up. I didn't want to argue because my landlord had already warned me about Blessing coming around and causing disturbances. The apartment walls were so thin that if a neighbor dropped a pin, I'd hear it, which meant they could hear our arguments, too. The landlord warned me that if Blessing caused any more trouble, he would get a no-trespass order against him. That's why I just let him rest and leave without further incident. Of course, we didn't discuss anything about the reason he came over in the first place.

The one good thing was that we didn't live in the same city—there was at least a 30- to 40-minute distance between us. I went to my bedroom with my baby to sleep, and while I was breastfeeding,

Blessing suddenly stormed in, looking very upset. I had no idea what was happening, but I got scared because I was holding my child. All I could think was that he wasn't going to get near me or my baby. As he approached, I kicked him in the stomach, still holding my baby with both hands. He stumbled and fell to the ground.

Then he got up and started screaming, "She stabbed me! She stabbed me! OMG, I'm bleeding, I'm losing a lot of blood, I'm dying! Someone help me!"

He then went to my brother's room and woke him up. I heard my brother telling him to call an ambulance, but Blessing refused and just kept screaming.

I was confused and tried to look at the carpet to see if there was blood, but there was nothing. So, I assumed it was one of his usual antics because, in the past, he had pulled something similar. I ignored it and went to bed. Later, while going to the bathroom, I saw him taking selfies on the couch. I didn't pay much attention and went back to bed.

Around 5 am, I heard a knock on my front door. I picked up my baby and went to check. I initially thought it was my landlord, coming because of the noise from the night before. I assumed Blessing had already left, which is why he didn't open the door. From the looks of the couch, it seemed he must have left.

I opened the door, and in front of me stood two police officers.

Police Officer 1 asked me, "Do you know Blessing?"

I affirmed, "Yes, I know him."

Then, Police Officer 1 asked me, "Where is he now?"

I honestly told them, "He was sleeping on that couch over there."

Police Officer 2 told me, "Blessing went to the emergency room with stab wounds. He told us you stabbed him."

"Okay! Okay! Hold on, officer, say what?" were my exact words.

They asked if they could come in, and since I thought I had nothing to hide, I said yes. They came in, looked around, and one went out. He came back a few minutes later with at least eight more officers.

The parking lot was lit up with blue lights, and my apartment was filled with forensic investigators, detectives, police officers—you name it. It felt like a scene from a movie was being produced live in my apartment. It felt like a long nightmare that I could not wake up from unless someone tapped me hard. They did not leave my premises until 10 am.

Then, it was DCF (Department of Children and Families) and DDS (Department of Disability Services). DDS had come for the client I was taking care of, and DCF came for my child and brother. Someone, please slap me out of this nightmare! The devil is real.

Glory to God that I had a family that is always there in good times and bad times. When my family heard about what was going on, they all came. I know you're asking yourself how they found out, right? I'll tell you. When Blessing was taking selfies, he posted on all his social media, stating that his baby's mama had stabbed him and ripped his stomach open, with food falling out.

The first person to see it was my brother, then my cousins, and so the phone calls followed. My aunt took my daughter so she wouldn't be put in the system, and my brothers stayed. Though DCF advised me to stay somewhere else so my brothers could remain in the apartment and continue school, I did as I was told and went to my cousin's place.

I recall everything like it was yesterday—the pain, the anger, the shame, the self-blaming. All I could say was, *"What have I done? How did I let this happen? If only I had walked away sooner."*

Yes, it was too late. The worst part was that my child was only four months old and breastfeeding. She had never tasted solid food until then. That night, I called to check on my baby, and the cry I heard was a cry I'll never forget. My breasts were so swollen from not breastfeeding. I cried continuously. I remember one of my cousin's friends calling her and asking if what he heard was true.

My cousin asked what he meant, and he said that everyone knew that I had stabbed someone, and he always knew that one day I would kill someone. That statement made me start doing a self-check on myself. From that day on, I stopped eating and felt like a failure. For once, I acknowledged that I was meant to be a nobody.

The following day, my cousin, who was staying at my place, called me and told me that the sheriff stopped by to serve me papers, but since I was not there, he left his card for me to call him back. I took the sheriff's number and called him right away, explaining that I wasn't there because DCF advised me to stay away so my brothers wouldn't be removed from the apartment. He informed me that he had come to serve me, but since I was in a different county, he would get back to me. I said okay and didn't worry much about it.

The following day, which was a Thursday, I had to visit my child. I was so excited about the visit. I got there, and everything went well. They even let me breastfeed. On my way out after the visit, a police officer at the door stopped me and asked for my identification. I asked the officer if everything was okay while giving him my ID. He looked at it and told me there was a warrant issued against me.

I was confused and asked him why. He explained that because the sheriff came to serve me and I wasn't at my premises, he went to court, and they issued a warrant for my arrest. No wonder he said he would get back to me. They cuffed me on the spot, put me in the cruiser, and took me to the county jail. They told me that it was a miscommunication, and that a family member could bail me out later. This was in the evening, so everything was closing for the day. After intake, I waited in that cold place, freezing.

Around 4 am, a very sweet, kind police lady came and asked me if I had killed someone. I said, "No, why?" She explained that my bail bond was over $150,000. I thought to myself, *no wonder nobody bailed me out.*

Early in the morning, they transported us to court and locked us in the back. While waiting, an attorney came by and asked for me. He said that my family had requested his help. I explained again what had happened, and we went to court together. He represented me, and the judge asked that I be released, but we had to go to the District Court to clear up the issue with the warrant.

It was Friday, and we all know that's the day everyone looks forward to the weekend, but if jailed, nothing can be done until Monday. Finally, when I was called before the judge, I walked in and saw my mom sitting, waiting for me. I could read the pain and tears in her eyes. The judge looked at me and apologized in advance, saying, "I am so sorry, ma'am, but the victim called and said that since he is still in the area, we should hold you until he leaves because not only are you a danger to him but to society."

And he did exactly that. He asked the police officer to take me in. Of course, they came and cuffed both my wrists and legs, taking me away in front of my mother. It took about two hours of waiting before we arrived at the correctional facility. In the truck, I met a young lady, and we started talking. She asked me what I had done. I told her everything, and she kept telling me that I'd be okay. She suggested I might serve three to six months tops.

"No," I kept telling her, "I can't afford to serve even a week because I'm innocent."

She told me she was doing two years because she stabbed her husband 24 times. Bless God, the man was alive and even visiting her in jail with the kids.

That's not my fate. The thought of my child visiting me in jail was just unacceptable. We finally arrived at the prison, and reality started sinking in. Yes, I was in jail. They did the intake, then the screening, and then the worst experience of my life happened. They had to check our body cavities, both front and back, to make sure we weren't hiding any drugs.

I was very humiliated because I had lost so much weight. I was probably weighing 90 lbs. You could see and count every rib on me. I had no flesh to cover my bones at all, and this was done while we were stripped naked. After that, they handed me the orange suit, socks, and a blanket, and of course, I was taken to my room.

What a nightmare!

A JOURNEY OF FAITH AND REDEMPTION

I t's not easy, people. So, yes, I did wear the orange suit, and it absolutely did not look good on me at all.

County jails are nothing compared to prison, and here's why: at least in the county jail, you expect to be bailed out, and there's no orange suit or getting naked while correction officers watch and inspect your body, even after you've gone through two screening machines. They still do it manually. Immediately after that, they took us to our lock-up room, which had one bunk bed. I chose the bottom bed because I was by myself then.

Later, they came and took me to test for drugs and to pump my breasts. When I came back, they had brought in a young lady who was nine months pregnant. I asked her why she was in, and she told me that her boyfriend had gone and taken back the bail.

That's when I realized that my situation wasn't as bad as I thought. This lady knew she was going to have her baby in jail, and DCF would take her baby away immediately. At least I had the opportunity to take care of my child for a few months, and I was hoping that things would work out for me to get out.

That Friday night, I started thinking about how I ended up there. Putting the pieces together made me realize that, while I might have been innocent, it was partly my fault as well. There were certain things I had to change in my life. They did their checks twice—at midnight and 4 am. Breakfast was at 5 am. I never had a chance to eat; all I could do was cry. I think it was Sunday when I tried to have lunch, but I couldn't bring myself to eat. I had lost all my appetite.

All I could think about was my family and how my child was suffering because of me. The showers were horrible, and the water made your skin so dry. They didn't offer any lotion or body wash. Unfortunately for me, Monday was a holiday, so I had to wait until Tuesday to go back to court. I hadn't slept for the nights I was there. Monday night, I kept thinking about the whole situation, and it dawned on me that, in this situation, I had no one to get me out of it. I thought about my past and the kind of life I was living and realized that I had to do something different.

I remember asking God for help, "God, I have heard about you and the things you can do. I have heard your stories with Moses and all that. So, I'll make a deal with you: if you take me out of this situation, I promise I will change. I will serve you for the rest of my life, and I will dedicate my child to you."

That was it, and now I had to wait until morning. Even then, I just kept thinking about what my fate would be. At one point, I was okay with doing three to six months as long as I could leave and have my child back. But again, I had some relief and hope. I can't exactly explain it, but I knew something in me had changed, lessened, or been taken away.

They woke us up at 5 am to get ready for court. I took my shower, and we had to wait up front for the van to pick us up. I was so skinny that the correction officer made a joke, saying they should make handcuffs for kids since the ones they had were too big for me. Anyway, we got to court around 9 am and had to wait to be called. I think I was the last person for the day. My hearing started at 3 pm and went on till 5 pm. All I remember was the judge looking at me and asking them to release me without any bail but with conditions and a restraining order to stay away from Blessing. I was also required to do random alcohol testing since Blessing told the police that I was an alcoholic.

I fell to the ground in court and started crying. I asked the judge again if I was going home, and she confirmed. I cried more while kneeling on the floor, saying, "So you exist? So, you do hear prayers? So you are God, and you are real?"

That's all I kept saying. My mom started crying, and eventually, I was able to see the outside world after four days of incarceration.

On Wednesday, I met with my attorney to go through the upcoming cases. I had two of them: one for custody of my child and the criminal one. Did I mention that my record said, "Assault with Intent to Murder"?

Yes!

When I got home, the first thing I did was take a nice long shower and try to eat something. It was my first time back in the apartment, and it felt different. My brothers were there, but my child was not. I became depressed, and all I did was sleep and cry for the first few days.

That night, I watched Joel Osteen and got saved officially on TV. I said the sinner's prayer about 100 times, just in case I didn't do it right the first 50 times. I also started my church hunting, looking for a place where I could fellowship for the rest of my life. I was trying to keep my part of the agreement with God since He had fulfilled His part.

There were about four churches around my neighborhood. I tried all of them but felt like I didn't fit in. Then, one of my very good friends introduced me to a church she was attending. It had just opened around the same time my case started. When I went there, I felt at home immediately, so I embraced my new beginning with God.

I told the pastor about my covenant with God and that I needed to dedicate my child ASAP. When God is at work, the devil cannot stand the fire. I started seeing and experiencing positive results from serving God.

The Bible says, "No mere man has ever seen, heard or even imagined what wonderful things God has ready for those who love the Lord." God, in his own special and unique ways, was at work in my life. He started constructing me from the inside.

Proverbs 3:5-6 says *"Trust in the Lord with all your heart And lean not on your own understanding. In all your ways, acknowledge him, and he will direct your paths."*

I did; I decided to try Jesus willingly and asked him to direct my path. I started holding onto his word because *Psalms 138:2* says *God honors his word above all his name.*

He then says in *Deuteronomy 7:9,* *"Therefore, know that the Lord your God, the faithful God who keeps covenant and mercy for a thousand generations with those who love him and keep his commandments."*

I had nothing to lose in trusting in God. The church chose a date, and my child was dedicated. What a glorious day it was; my baby was the first dedicated in the new church, but also in my family. Hmmm…the devil was losing a battle, slowly.

Oh, taste and see that the Lord is good; Blessed is the man who trusts in Him! *Psalms 34:8.*

The Lord was being so good to me, and my faith was growing every day.

The attorney needed $7,000 for my criminal case and $2,000 for custody to start. I only had $400 in my account. But God! He used my family to support me during that period. They were sending money from left and right so that I was able to pay the attorney.

Not to mention, I had lost my job with the state, so I had to start job hunting. This was something I hadn't done in years because I had been at my previous job for over 5 years. Looking for a job wasn't so much of a problem, but I thought getting hired because of my CORI was going to be an issue.

I applied for a few positions in the healthcare field. How God did it, I cannot explain. What I do know is that for every job I applied to, they interviewed me and wanted to hire me.

Has anyone ever read a book called "God's Smuggler"?

In the book, the writer tells how he smuggled Bibles into a country where it wasn't allowed. Every time he reached the border, he prayed for God to make the border patrols overlook what they were supposed to see, much like how my CORI was covered. The jobs I got were going to pay me double what I used to earn. If that's not God, then I don't know what is. My father in heaven promised to be with me and comfort me.

Psalms 23:4 says, *"Yea, though I walk through the valley of the shadow of death, I will fear no evil; For you are with me; Your rod and your staff, they comfort me."*

Philippians 4:19 tells me, *"And my God shall supply all my needs according to his riches in glory by Christ Jesus."*

"Yes," I said, "My God" and "My needs," not "your needs," because I know the God I serve. I secured two jobs, one in the morning and one in the evening, at different places but under one agency. On my first day of orientation at my evening job, I passed out and fell into a trash can, causing panic among my coworkers. The next morning, my employer called all my references again just to ensure that I didn't use drugs.

From Depression to Divine Deliverance

I was still battling depression; I barely ate and lost a significant amount of weight. I went from 90 lbs to about 88 lbs. I needed money for the lawyer, for my child, for the bills, and most importantly, I wanted my child back home. During the dedication ceremony, he was not yet back home, so I asked my family to bring him to church for me. It was a leap of faith because my family did not attend church at all, but by God's grace, they all came for the sake of my child. I cannot praise God enough. Who else but Jesus could perform such a miracle?

After that night, my employer started calling me anorexic, implying I had an eating disorder involving bingeing and purging. God forbid, I was not anorexic; I was simply a woman struggling with inner pain and depression that only God could truly understand. The legal cases drained me, along with the classes that DCF required me to complete before regaining custody of my child, and, of course, managing two jobs. On my days off, I attended these classes, which were in-person back then since virtual meetings weren't widely adopted yet due to the pandemic.

DCF gave me an action plan that included domestic violence counseling, alcohol and drug evaluations, a psychological evaluation, parenting classes, therapy, and anger management. Additionally, I had to appear in court twice a week for both juvenile and criminal cases, and undergo random alcohol testing every week. These requirements posed a significant challenge; I had to call a designated number every morning after 6 am to check if my color was selected. If it was, I had to go to court for testing, sometimes twice a week, forcing me to rearrange my daily schedule.

The criminal case kept getting postponed every time we went to court for various reasons. What frustrated me most was that my attorney started charging $425 for each meeting. Since we were meeting twice a week for both cases, I was paying him nearly $1000 per week.

The juvenile court case concluded swiftly. God manifested Himself, turning the evil intended against me into good. Blessing lost his job, housing, and car, making it impossible for him to attend court in the final days. Earlier, he had even asked DCF for financial assistance or gas vouchers, claiming the courthouse was too far from his residence, about a 30-minute drive. He eventually stopped showing up in court, citing one excuse after another.

Part of the action plan required a stable home, which Blessing did not have. In an attempt to deceive DCF, he paid an elderly woman to pose as his grandmother during their inspections. When DCF raised concerns about this in court, I was stunned because I knew his actual grandmother had passed away when he was young. When questioned by my attorney, he admitted he referred to elderly individuals as "grandma" or "grandpa" regardless of blood relation.

During a subsequent visit by DCF, the elderly woman was replaced by another claiming to be Blessing's aunt. His attempts to manipulate the situation became apparent. DCF discovered there was no familial relationship between them. Despite all his efforts, the case quickly concluded, and I was finally reunited with my daughter. Truly, God's intervention was evident throughout.

So finally, that was done with, and I got full custody of my child, Praise the Lord my people. The word of the Lord says in **1 Thessalonians 5: 16-18**. *Rejoice always, pray continually, give thanks in all circumstances; for this is God's will for you in Christ Jesus.* Now, I was left dealing with the criminal case, which had been repeatedly postponed for years. Finally, they scheduled the case for trial. By then, I was in a much better place spiritually, mentally, and financially.

God was blooming and showing his glory for me. I was receiving every promised blessing in **Deuteronomy 28**. I am saying this with no doubt,(*The word of God is alive and active, sharper than a two-edged sword, piercing even to the division of soul and spirit, and of joints and marrow and is a discerner of the thoughts and intents of the heart.* **Hebrews 4:12**). *Romans 8:28. And we know that all things work together for good to those who love God, to those who are the called according to his purpose.*

In Christ, life began to make sense profoundly. I became a new creation. I won't say that salvation is easy—it's actually a challenging journey. But by God's grace, He empowers us to achieve victory through Him. Through His grace, we learn that God goes before us, He is with us, He never leaves us or forsakes us, and He commands us not to fear or be dismayed (*Deuteronomy 31:8*).

As I embraced my faith, I started facing more attacks from the enemy than ever before. It's true what they say—that a thief doesn't rob an empty house. Once you choose Jesus, the devil unleashes all his agents to fight against you, aiming to hinder you from recognizing and fulfilling your calling.

The Holy Spirit gently stirred within me a desire to pray, and in Christ Jesus, my spiritual growth blossomed. I devoted most of my time to church, ensuring I didn't miss a single day—even when the enemy threatened me with sickness, I resolved to die on the altar if need be. Over time, I was appointed a leader in my church, and installed as the chief intercessor. I embraced this responsibility with passion, understanding my assignment and serving God wholeheartedly. My life found its true meaning with God at its center.

During this period, I battled with the craving for alcohol. There were days when the desire was so intense that I found myself driving to the liquor store. But I give all credit to the Holy Spirit; truly, God is faithful. As soon as I reached the parking lot, the internal struggle began anew.

One would tell me to go ahead; the Hennessy or Tequila would make me feel better. It would even tell me I can opt for a Roscato.

Then the Holy Spirit would remind me," *Therefore, if anyone is in Christ, he is a new Creation; old things have passed away; behold all things have become new.*" ***2 Corinthians 5:17***.

The Spirit of addiction had been lifted from me, but I wasn't yet fully delivered from its influence. This meant the devil would still attempt to exploit my vulnerability. From my past experiences, I've learned that the devil uses various tactics for the same issues; he's not particularly clever. We often give him opportunities through our words and actions. Dear Sisters and Brothers, it's important to note that he can never attack you through a stranger—no way!

A COURTROOM MIRACLE

A good example is that you can never hate someone you don't know; it's usually those who are close to you and may have offended you in some way. Similarly, the devil attacks in a similar manner. He starts with you, and if you overcome him, he moves on to those close to you—your children, family members, friends, or co-workers. He always circles back to exploit your weaknesses because that's his only way to attack. For me, he targets what used to be my vulnerabilities, triggering cravings for alcohol, especially when I'm angry.

But since God's grace is sufficient *2 Corinthians 12:9*, the criminal case continued. They dropped the charges from assault with intent to murder to assault with a dangerous weapon on a family member. I told my attorney that Blessing was not my family member and we were not married; the only thing we had in common was our child. So, the charges were reduced to assault with a dangerous weapon.

As time went by, my attorney asked for a trial. However, the trial didn't start right away because of COVID-19, and everything began happening on Zoom. Finally, after a while, they set a date.

The day of the trial came, and it was just me and my little brother. My family had relocated out of state, so if anything were to happen, I would have no one with me. We walked into court that morning and met with my attorney. The first thing he asked for was his money. We paid him and then went into the courtroom. It took about an hour to select the jurors and go through the procedures of dos and don'ts.

After that process was completed, they gave us a few minutes to prepare. We went out, and that's when my attorney suggested he was going to request another court date. After all these years and so much payment, he wanted to ask for another date. I firmly said no and asked him why. His excuse was that he realized the district attorney had more evidence than he did. I asked him what happened to all the evidence I gave him, including the ones from the juvenile case. He didn't answer me. You can imagine my annoyance. Then he started telling me that I was going to go to jail. What audacity!

We went back in, and my attorney reminded me that he would not put me on the stand. All the witnesses were called; I only had my brother as my witness, and of course, the police officers who came to my apartment that day. They were not really my witnesses or his but the state's. Before the trial started, my attorney complained about the evidence that the DA had, so the DA told my attorney that he was going to throw away all the evidence except for the recording. Yes, when Blessing started the drama, he was also recording at the same time. In the recording, he is shouting about how he is bleeding to death, and no one is helping him.

So that's all the jury needed. Unfortunately, from my end, the judge said that my attorney had not produced any evidence, including the recording they gave him from the other court. I was furious to hear that I did not produce any evidence. The judge's exact words were, "I do not want to hear any excuse from you because this case has lingered for years, and you did not produce any evidence from her or for her."

My attorney was speechless; he had nothing to say after that. After the hearing, the jury found me guilty. They pronounced me GUILTY. My heart dropped. To make matters worse, when the judge asked the DA what he was proposing, he said I should be sentenced to two years in the corrections facility.

My heart sank. I remember the words I silently said in my heart: "No, God, that cannot happen. I cannot go back to prison. The only reason I will go back is with my Bible, and it will be to preach your word. I told God there is no way you brought me out; let me serve you, let me pray for others, only for you to send me back. God, I refuse. Just like Daniel in the den of lions, you are going to fight for me now."

The judge lifted the gavel, and just as he was about to bring it down, he put it back and said, "Mom, can you come here, please? Ever since the case started, I have never had you speak." I slowly walked to where the judge was. He asked me to explain what led to that moment.

He added, "I know you went through domestic violence, and that man is a lousy father. I would never want him to raise a child, but can you please explain to me what happened?"

Before I opened my mouth to speak, I felt a gentle tap on my left shoulder, with a gentle voice saying, "Be still and know that I am God."

I explained to the judge the events that led to that moment. When I finished, he looked at the DA and the jurors and shook his head. Then he said, "No, she will not serve any time nor pay any fees. I am a father and I have daughters, and I would never want any of my daughters to experience what she has experienced."

Then he looked at me and said, "Mom, go home to your child." Come on now, tell me, if that is not God, then who? Forget that I was in court; I started going back and forth, thanking God and speaking in tongues. Nothing was going to stop me from glorifying Him.

By the time we were leaving the courtroom, my attorney was nowhere to be found. It was like he had just vanished. I didn't care really; victory was mine. The devil had just lost another battle because, from the beginning, the battle belonged to Him, *1 Samuel 17:47*. On our way home, my brother told me that when the DA suggested the two years in a correctional facility, he was thinking of how he would stop his life and take care of my child. But who is God?

How God planned that day amazed me because, on my way to church, I recalled that as a church, it was our fasting day for evening prayers. I had not told anyone from church that I had a trial that day, but when I walked into my Father's house that evening, I understood the love, the mercy, and the grace of God. The word says that His mercies are renewed every morning *Lamentations 3:22*.

REDEMPTION

I walked into the sanctuary and headed straight to the altar. By God's grace, I was the one leading prayer that night. I had never felt God's presence so close as I did that evening. After that, I hugged my pastors in tears and explained to them the events of that day. Another worship session started all over. I must say that I can't and will never get enough of God. He is too sweet. If you were me, wouldn't you serve God with your all? My life is not mine; I live it for God, for His work and kingdom. Whatever I do, I can't repay God for all He has done for me. There is no perfect present for Him except to offer myself daily as a living sacrifice.

In all this, God was very faithful, and out of that season, I learned a couple of lessons, especially for young ladies, single mothers, and those going through or who have undergone domestic violence. You cannot change a full-grown man unless he wants to change. We have an African saying that you can't bend a tree when it's fully grown; it will break. As humans, we can only change if we accept accountability and realize we need help. You cannot send a person to see a doctor if they don't know they are sick; they can only decide when it's time to go for a check-up. Never even think that getting pregnant for a man will make him change. That's exactly what I thought, that because I was carrying his first child, he was going to change.

Don't get me wrong; some people can check into their flaws and decide to become better, or by God's grace, which will take a lot of prayer, fasting, and sacrifice. A salvation package is a bundle that one can't do without the other, and in this case, you must be willing to give it your all. I was taught that the best way to know a man is by the way he treats his mother and sister. If he does not treat his family right, then you must be very careful. But the truth be told, if he or she reveals the red flags, run before it is too late. Don't hold on, don't doubt your instincts, don't be scared, don't be embarrassed, or worry about what's next. There is help and resources out there for people like you and me. The only worry you can have is for you and your children. Are you ready to raise your kids in that environment?

The outcome is that whether it's your son, he may decide to emulate his father, and if it's a daughter, she may choose to endure in her relationship as her mother did. This is why we have so many broken homes, because children grow up using excuses like "I grew up in a broken home" or "My mom stayed and raised us."

Please don't. Choose yourself and love yourself before you love someone else. Value yourself because you are priceless. Your worth doesn't have a set price tag; why do I say that? Because from the day you were born until the woman you have become now, it took a lot of resources, pain, laughter, victories, failures, sickness, and more. So why rate yourself so low?

Another lesson I learned from my experiences was that when God wants to use you, He often isolates you first. Why? Because when you are not isolated, there is too much noise around for you to discern your Father's voice. I encourage every believer reading this to utilize their quiet time effectively. As a mom, it has always been challenging for me to find quiet time, so I've found that the best time to listen to my Father is when everyone else has gone to bed.

Later, during the healing process, I began to think: what if he had died? Or what if my child had been hurt in the process? What if the knife had struck me? Right now, I might be facing charges of manslaughter, murder, or worse. I can't bear to think about how I would live with that, and for that, I will never take my blessings for granted. Even in that moment, He was there, and He fought for me. I mean, how would my child grow up without a mom or dad? There's so much that comes to mind about that day, and all I can see is "But God." I don't know about you, but I was given a fresh start, a chance to be redeemed and restored.

I ask God to speak to me when my mind is at rest, when there's nothing else but my spirit for Him to work with. He can speak or reveal Himself through dreams, and I'm able to understand the messages. Through all this, I have learned to recognize my Father's voice, so even now, if He speaks in the midst of chaos, I can discern His voice.

When I was in jail, alone for three days with nothing to do but listen to my thoughts, salvation came out of that isolation. It was then that I realized God had been seeking my attention for so long, but because of my pride, I had missed my chance with Him. Now

I understand why He met with Moses at the burning bush *Exodus 3:1-6*, and why He asked Abraham to leave his family and go to the land He would show him *Genesis 12:1-3*. These examples continue.

God doesn't work with the righteous or the perfect; no, He came and died for the unrighteous, to give new names to those rejected by the world, those whom people think are destined for nothing. All I know now is that God is able; He turns ashes into beauty. He doesn't operate with human logic but with His divine wisdom. He is unique and supreme, unchanging yet forgiving and merciful. Who else but God? If you choose Him, He guarantees victory in every situation. The only times He says "no" are for our protection. Sometimes, we may not understand Him, but what kind of Father would He be if He allowed us to get into trouble?

The book of James tells us that God does not tempt us but allows us to be tested, and in every test, He provides a way out. It also teaches us to count it all joy when we face trials, knowing that the testing of our faith produces patience. I acknowledge God in both the good and the bad because I know that I had a choice. I chose to sin without anyone forcing me; every wrong choice I made had its consequences. Someone once said, "You have the right to make a choice but not to choose the consequences."

Looking back now, I wouldn't want it any other way. Every good and bad experience I went through has shaped who I am today. I'm not suggesting we take advantage of God's mercy or sin, knowing He is merciful or because of His unconditional love. God knows our lives from the day we were born until the day we die. Is He willing to protect us from the devil and keep us safe? Yes, He is, and that's why He offers us salvation. His sacrifice for us is the ultimate expression of love. Few parents would take a bullet for their children, but God did it for each of us, regardless of race or tribe.

SALVATION

Before I received salvation, sinning felt satisfying, especially when it brought fear or respect from others. What never crossed my mind was God's promises and the consequences of sin. God fulfills His promises to us when we love, honor, and obey Him. The devil, on the other hand, deceives. Sin leads to trouble, and even if you avoid consequences in this life, it leads to spiritual separation from God.

Salvation comes with tests, but God is faithful to guide us through. In contrast, the devil abandons and shames. Any agreement with Satan leads to pain; he offers no true victory or lasting fulfillment. For example, stealing may bring temporary gain but carries lasting consequences—jail, probation, or worse, eternal separation from God.

It wasn't about my family; the devil exploited my weaknesses and used family members as conduits. The spirit of alienation led me to seek solace outside my home, where addiction to alcohol took hold.

Unlike God, Satan doesn't reveal sin all at once; he introduces it in small doses that grow and spread, affecting entire generations if unchecked. My biggest mistake was listening to the voices that told me I was hated, unworthy, and filled with lies. Satan exploits our weaknesses—like self-doubt, seeking wrong resources like witchcraft, and ancestral patterns—to torment those unaware of Christ.

During my darkest times, facing court issues, my mother sought solutions through witchcraft. I don't blame her; I love her deeply for standing by me, though misguided. Humans love to play the blame game when we fail, yet God provides answers through His word and the Holy Spirit, our faithful helper who never fails. Aligning with the Holy Spirit as a believer is invaluable; he guides, protects, corrects, and assures us like no other.

There's a void without the Holy Spirit; life lacks meaning. From the beginning, God has sustained me. I'm a work-in-progress believer, alive only by His grace. I've learned life's hard lessons and refuse to exploit the Gospel. The devil constantly reminds me of my past, using even the church to hinder the spread of the gospel.

I share my experiences to inspire those who feel hopeless or worthless. Life is beautiful, and rewarding, and God promises never to abandon us. Trust, believe, and love again; our past prepares us for the future. Don't let it define you; Jesus erased those charges. Grow like a seed, pushing through the darkness to blossom. Just as a plant grows twice—above and below ground—the deeper the roots, the stronger it stands.

We choose growth or stagnation. In abuse, you may not know if it will end or cost your life. As a domestic violence counselor,

I've heard many stories where objects were hurled, leading to tragic outcomes. Be the seed that seeks rain and sunlight, rising to survive and thrive. Your struggles are your strength; your test, a testimony to change lives.

God's plan for you surpasses what you imagine. Live up to your calling despite obstacles. Ignore the negative voices; declare victory and lift your head high.

After everything Satan put you through, my sister, what's new? Now, you can look back, smile, and tell him you've transformed. More importantly, what legacy will you leave for your generation? If you're still alive, there's work left to do. If God wakes you up each day, it's because you have a mission to fulfill. Will you keep making excuses or trust God to show you the way? Remember, it's not about you but the One who created you. If you continue like this, God might grow weary and call you home. Are you prepared to die tonight? If not, or if you have doubts or fear, you're not ready. That means you're living an empty life. Start living for Christ, a life worthy before God, because life is spiritual. Everything I endured was due to an open door for demons to access.

Angels and demons surround us; Earth revolves around the prince of the air. Running away, pride, arrogance, sex, stealing— all are spirits; some passed down from our parents unwittingly. The good news is nothing surprises God; everything we do or live through existed before. The only one surprised is the devil when we get saved, baptized, and delivered.

When you choose salvation, you declare war on the devil because he knows the power and anointing you carry. He'll do everything to stop or delay your destiny, just as he did to me. So, shall we take up this battle and let God lead? I'm tired of this demon stealing, killing, and destroying lives, including our children. Will you sit and blame situations, or will you act?

Fight spiritually; let's unite to stop his mission. Shut down the works of witches in our cities, homes, and lives. Silence his plans for our marriages and reject his lies of inadequacy. The battle is the Lord's, but He waits for us to use our power so He can release His ability. We receive not because we ask not. Remember, do not underestimate the power of midnight prayers; witches know its potency.

Step out of addiction, abuse, and rejection. Sister, you are worthy. God had a plan for you before your birth. Know that God created you, and for every challenge, He is God, our Abba Father. Restore your faith, rededicate your life to Him, surrender all, and He will do for you as He did for me. Don't fear tomorrow; trust Him in each moment. We have 365 days in a year, and the Bible tells us, *"Do not fear"* 365 times—a word for every doubt.

It's okay, sister. God will make a way; try Him, then share your testimony. I speak from experience—I am a living testimony. My mom and I are now best friends; we have our moments, but with God in control, I fear nothing. I cherish my scars and cherish my relationship with my children. All I went through made me better, and I'm grateful to my abuser, my blessing in disguise. Yes, I love

Blessing—no hurt feelings; without him, God wouldn't have saved me.

And my final encouragement is learning how to forgive—it's a very difficult thing, especially for someone who took everything away from you. The good thing is, that God is a rewarder who not only rewards but multiplies. Forgiving is not for your enemy but for your heart, soul, and spirit. When you forgive, you conquer, and the enemy loses. You free yourself and embrace a new self.

If no one loves you, let God love you, and then love yourself. If no one buys you flowers, buy them for yourself. Aren't you living for yourself? If they don't take you out, treat yourself to a massage, facial, or a movie with your kids. Dress for yourself and be happy in your own skin. Look in the mirror and appreciate yourself, because God took serious time to put you together. God does not make mistakes; we are everything He intended us to be, except for the sinning part. The good news is we can repent and seek God's mercy.

Dear Sister,

Forgiving is like getting rid of poison that may have caused you depression, anxiety, mood swings, and more. As a mom, forgiving helps you raise your kids right because they inherit DNA from both you and their dad. Occasionally, your child might do something that reminds you of your past. Instead of cursing or calling them names because of what you went through, smile at them and bless God for healing. Forgiving is a cure; it heals where it hurts most. Embrace life and cherish every moment; tomorrow is not promised to anyone. Some sleep and don't wake up, some leave home and never return due to accidents. So, live your life fulfilling God's purpose.

The only way to please God is by choosing Him, surviving temptation, surrendering, and giving Him all of us and everything connected to us. Everything we have is a bonus gift from God, and He can decide to take it all away. Can you still love Him with nothing? Can you still trust and love Him without a job, house, income, marriage, or children?

Like Job, can you still serve Him?

God knows our needs and desires, and He's ready to provide if we humble ourselves and serve in truth and spirit. We're on a journey that can end at any moment. Where have you invested your faith? What keeps you awake at night, for that's your idol? The best part of serving God is His provision; that's why we call Him Jehovah Jireh. In the Bible, all who trusted and invested in Him were abundantly blessed—ask Abraham, David, or Solomon. They lacked nothing.

So, don't you think that after sacrificing Himself to prove His love for you, He would abundantly provide for you? His love is unfailing, pure, and genuine. After years of feeling betrayed and doubting love, I encountered His love, and I love God. His love requires no effort or stress; all He asks for is a yes from you. Can you say yes today? Can you choose Him today, no matter what? Can you give Him a chance to transform your life, give you a new name, and change your story?

Can you allow Him to call you His own, the apple of His eye? Can you allow Him to show you glimpses of His glory? I pray that as you ask yourself these questions, you'll say yes. Don't wait until it's too late; don't hesitate or procrastinate. Just say yes, and all will be well. I live by these questions daily, and He has never forsaken me, not once.

To wrap up, not only am I saved, delivered, and redeemed, but I've also been sober for six years. I am a counselor, teacher, evangelist, and a product of heaven. God has done a wonderful work in me.

Be ready when He comes, for you don't want Him to reject you and say He doesn't know you. Our goal and vision are for heaven. I will continue to keep you in my prayers, that as we journey together, God will receive all the glory. Amen.

P.S. I love you, sis.

www.ingramcontent.com/pod-product-compliance
Lightning Source LLC
Chambersburg PA
CBHW051549120626
46551CB00013B/1438